I0143257

More Than Money

More Than Money

A STUDY OF THE SPIRITUAL
PRACTICE OF GENEROSITY

DARREN CUSHMAN WOOD

North United Methodist Church ● Indianapolis, IN

© 2023 North United Methodist Church, 3808 N. Meridian St., Indianapolis, IN 46208. NorthChurchIndy.com.

ISBN 978-1-7327761-7-3 (epub)

ISBN 978-1-7327761-8-0 (paperback)

The cover art comes from a small portion of one of the many beautiful banners throughout North United Methodist Church created by the late Doris Douglas, a long-time member, and other artists.

Biblical quotations from the New Revised Standard Version of the Bible, copyright © 1989 by the Division of Christian Education of the National Council of the Churches of Christ in the USA and used by permission.

Hymn quotations from The United Methodist Hymnal, copyright © 1989 by the United Methodist Publishing House and from The Faith We Sing, copyright © 2000 by Abingdon Press and used by permission.

Contents

Part I. Main Body

Introduction: What Is Generosity?

When you hear the word "generosity," what comes to mind? Is it a wealthy person who contributes vast sums of money to charity? Is it the spontaneous, warm feeling of sympathy for the less fortunate?

In their book "The Paradox of Generosity" (Oxford University Press, 2014), Christian Smith and Hilary Davidson define generosity as "the virtue of giving good things to others freely and abundantly.[1]" For centuries the word "generosity" applied only to the wealthy and their practices of giving, but by the 19th century it came to be seen as a character trait that anyone could acquire. It is called a "virtue" because it is a quality that is formed through intentional, habitual practice.

This understanding of generosity is very different from the stereotypes based on wealth and spontaneity. It is something that everyone can do, but it takes practice.

It is not the same as "altruism," which is a completely selfless concern for the well-being of others.

A person can be generous and be motivated by the benefits they receive as byproducts of their generosity.

On the other hand, generosity excludes any attempt to

manipulate or control through the giving of gifts. The end goal of generosity is the well-being of others.

Because generosity is the virtue of giving good things, it is much more than donating money. To be sure it includes financial gifts, but there are many other things that enhance the well-being of others. There is the generosity of our presence and relational support (emotional generosity); there is the sharing of our time and talents to help a neighbor (timely generosity); and there are the collective efforts of being generous that we do through the church and other organizations.

Smith and Davidson show the benefits of generosity for the giver. People who practice a lifestyle of emotional, timely, and financial generosity are happier and healthier, have a greater sense of purpose, and more fulfilling relationships. Indeed, acts of generosity

> *What reservations do I have about examining my generosity?*

and well-being are mutually reinforcing. Thus, they describe the practice of generosity as a paradox: "The reality of generosity is instead actually paradoxical. Generosity does not usually work in simple, zero-sum, win-lose ways. The results of generosity are often instead unexpected, counterintuitive, win-win[2]."

If you want a better quality of life, you have to do what Jesus said, "For those who want to save their life will lose it, and those who lose their life for my sake, and for the sake of the gospel, will save it. For what does it profit anyone to gain the whole world and forfeit their life?" (Mark 8:35-36)

This study guide is based on "The Paradox of Generosity."

I encourage you to get a copy and read it along with this study, especially if you are leading a discussion group. For readers of the book, you will notice that I have made some changes to the categories Smith and Davidson use to make them more useful for our reflections, but the basic concepts are the same.

Whether you are doing this with a small group or on your own, this study guide is designed to help you develop the spiritual practice of generosity. Each session features a generosity "audit" to aid your personal introspection, and a generosity "experiment" to put into practice the ideas for that session. A generosity "journal" is included at the end of each session for you to record your reflections and experiences.

Generosity is never an easy topic. We may feel uncomfortable because we assume that it only involves money. We may shy away from it because we feel inadequate to call ourselves "generous." Or we may not want to examine the deeper issues that it brings up about our relationships and priorities.

Taking on the issue of generosity is not for the fainthearted, but it is worth it. Learning to be more generous will enhance our relationships, deepen our faith, and improve our health. It is worth the investment.

1. **Emotional**
Generosity

INTRODUCTION

From music to athletics to academics, we know that practice is an essential part of becoming proficient. So too with generosity. In "The Paradox of Generosity," Notre Dame researchers Christian Smith and Hilary Davidson detail the psychological, interpersonal, and physical benefits of generosity for the giver. But they caution that "for generosity to enhance one's well-being it must be *practiced*.[3]" Random acts of generosity do not have a beneficial effect; instead, our formation as generous persons takes time, repetition, and practice.

Generosity is a spiritual practice because it enhances our connection with God, and through God's Spirit, with others. Jesus said, "For where your treasure is, there your heart will be also...No one can serve two masters; for a slave will either hate the one and love the other, or be devoted to the one and despise the other. You cannot serve God and wealth (Matthew

6:21, 22-23)." By focusing our treasures on God and others we reorient our lives to the source of our life and joy in Christ.

Our treasures are more than money. In this first session we examine "emotional generosity." This kind of generosity includes giving one's undivided attention to another person; making a special point to be kind to someone who is troubled; praying with and for others; expressing affirmation, and showing hospitality. This foundational form of generosity can also be called "relational" or "interpersonal" generosity.

As you begin your reflections, remember back across your life. When have you been the recipient of emotional generosity?

READINGS

2 Corinthians 1:3-7

What is the relationship between God's comfort for us and our comfort for others?

How did Paul see his "afflictions" as an aid to his ministry?

Have your "afflictions" made you more compassionate or more reticent toward others?

Who do you know is under pressure right now, and what might you do to be emotionally generous to them?

Job 2:11-13

What do Job's friends do and not do?

How do you know when to "just listen" rather than problem solve for someone in need?

Psalm 31

When have you experienced God walking with you during a time of serious distress?

How can we imitate God's readiness to listen?

EMOTIONAL GENEROSITY AUDIT

In the past 30 days:[4]

When one of my loved ones needed my attention, I really tried to slow down and give them the time and help they needed.   **Y   N**

I went the "extra mile" to help take care of my friends, relatives, and acquaintances.   **Y   N**

When friends or family members experienced something upsetting or discouraging, I made a special point of being kind to them.   **Y   N**

I was willing to risk my own feelings being hurt in the process if I stood a chance of helping someone else in need.   **Y   N**

I made it a point to let my friends and family know how much I love and appreciate them.   **Y   N**

I went out of my way to take time to include someone at work/church/school who was new or overlooked.   **Y**   **N**

If you answered no to any of these statements, what interfered with your ability to be emotionally generous?

GENEROSITY EXPERIMENT ONE

This week, review those items in your audit that were "no." Try to find ways to practice each of them this week.

How did it make you feel?

How did your emotional generosity affect others?

2. **Timely Generosity**

INTRODUCTION

According to Steve Jobs, "My favorite things in life don't cost any money. It's really clear that the most precious resource we all have is time." Regardless of your financial situation, you can still be generous with your time. Timely generosity is not a consolation prize; it is a supreme act of generosity because it requires personal investment and relationship building.

10

Timely generosity is the Golden Rule — "Love your neighbor as yourself," (Leviticus 19:18, Romans 13:9) — put into action. It includes informal acts of helping a neighbor, such as watching their pet while they are on vacation, loaning them a gardening tool, or helping with a project. Timely generosity also

Did you know?

Americans who never:
● helped a friend or neighbor with a task: 30%
● watched the home of a friend: 34%
● took care of others' children: 42%
● donated blood: 88.5%

Source: "The Paradox of Generosity" by Christian Smith and Hilary Davidson, Oxford University Press.

includes a host of volunteer opportunities with non-profit organizations, civic groups, and churches[5]. Regardless of your skills, it is your willingness to lend a hand that makes all the difference.

When was the last time you were the recipient of timely generosity?

READINGS

Romans 13:8-10

The preceding passage (vv. 1-7) describes the Christian's relationship with the governing authorities. How is loving your neighbor a part of the Christian witness in society?

What is the relationship between the Ten Commandments and the Golden Rule?

Why is it difficult for us to love our neighbors?

Leviticus 19:13-18

In which areas of life does Leviticus apply the Golden Rule?

What kind of society does Leviticus envision?

What is the relationship between love and justice?

Psalm 146

How does the psalm describe God?

How is the nature of God the basis for loving our neighbors?

GENEROSITY AUDIT

In the past 30 days have you...

Taken care of another person's child **Y**   **N**

Watched the house/property of a friend/neighbor **Y**   **N**

Helped a coworker when it was not a part of your assigned tasks **Y**   **N**

Helped a friend or neighbor with a task **Y**   **N**

Assisted a stranger with information or a task **Y**   **N**

Helped a sick friend   **Y**   **N**

Other acts of timely generosity: _____

How much time do you spend each day...

Engaged in timely generosity _____

Watching TV _____

Online/engaged in social media _____

Doing a hobby _____

GENEROSITY EXPERIMENT TWO

This week, are there opportunities to turn any of your "nos" into "yeses?" Offer your time and skill to help a neighbor or a coworker solve a concrete problem.

What was the task?

How long did it take?

What was their reaction?

3. Financial Generosity

INTRODUCTION

How do numbers make you feel?

Some people like the orderliness and certainty of numbers. Mathematical proofs can be called "elegant."

> **Did you know?**
>
> ● Percentage of Americans who give 10% or more of their income: 2.7%
> ● Percentage of Americans who give less than 2% of their income: 86.2%
> ● Percentage of Americans who give 0% of their income: 44.8%
>
> *Source: "The Paradox of Generosity" by Christian Smith and Hilary Davidson, Oxford University Press.*

For others numbers are anxiety producing and baffling, especially when the numbers are dollars and cents. When it comes to finances, some people find security in a close scrutiny of their numbers. Others ignore the numbers altogether.

This week take a closer look at your financial generosity. The goal is to avoid the two temptations mentioned above. While there is no ultimate security in money, it is not something we should ignore either. We call it "currency" for good reason: money conveys our relationships, obligations, hopes and fears. In short, it is one form of currency of the soul.

On the positive side, God uses our financial resources as a currency of blessing to others. In turn, we are blessed through these relationships.

On the negative side, our financial resources can become a currency of unfaithfulness, expressing our lack of faith in God to care for us and our unwillingness to follow Christ. Ultimately our anxiety over money and our attachment to the things money can buy separates us from God.

Because it is a currency of good or ill, John Wesley counseled in his sermon "The Use of Money" that we should earn all we can, save all we can, and give all we can. The early Methodists became good at the first two, but they seemed to struggle with the last one.

In a series of sermons near the end of his life, Wesley warned them about the ill effects of wealth. Without a robust and systematic approach to giving, one's spiritual life is stunted.

Smith and Davidson's research backs up Wesley's maxim. If you want a healthier, happier, and more purpose-driven life, you need to practice generosity.

Take this week to review your practices of financial generosity. Make plans to earn all you can and save all you can so that you can give all you can.

When have you been the recipient of financial generosity?

What impact did it have?

How did/does it make you feel?

READINGS

Luke 21:1-4

What made her gift acceptable?

What would be a financial sacrifice for you?

What would you have to change or plan in order to do it?

I Samuel 25:14-25, 32-35

What motivated Abigail's generosity?

What character traits of Abigail does the story reveal?

How do you prioritize your financial giving? Which organizations and what amounts?

Psalm 116

What motivates the psalmist to "pay my vows to the Lord?" (v.14)

Which of the following motivates your giving to the church (rank from 1 to 4):

___ Gratitude for God's love
___ Duty to God
___ Support the mission of the church

___ Thankful for your church family

GENEROSITY AUDIT

Look at your total financial giving (include all organizations, not just the church. Also include other informal financial gifts to family and friends which are not loans).

What percentage of your net income is it?

What do your financial gifts reveal about your values and priorities?

What would you like to change?

GENEROSITY EXPERIMENT THREE

This Monday, begin keeping a record of every potential opportunity to give away $10.

On Friday, choose one of these opportunities and make your donation.

How many opportunities did you record?

4. The Generous Church

INTRODUCTION

Nestled among the oaks and pine trees in Summerville, S.C. is Dorchester Presbyterian Church. My father-in-law, Richard Cushman, was the founding pastor, and for over 30 years led the congregants in becoming a generous church.

There are four buildings that house the sanctuary, day care, fellowship hall and offices. Each one was built by volunteer crews of church members over the course of 30 years.

Behind the church are several acres of woodlands that the church maintains as a nature preserve amid several subdivisions.

Dorchester is an example of the generous church. Its members shared their time and talents to physically and spiritually build the church and its mission. They share their generosity with God's creation and the community.

The generous church is more than a fiscally sound congregation. To be sure, financial sharing is a necessary part of the life of the congregation, but as you have learned from the previous sessions, generosity is more than money.

Did you know?

● 89% of volunteers report that volunteering has improved their sense of well-being
● 73% of volunteers report that volunteering has lowered their stress levels

Source: "The Paradox of Generosity" by Christian Smith and Hilary Davidson, Oxford University Press.

The generosity of the church is a reaction to God's generosity. The church is created by grace. The gift of the Holy Spirit connects us with one another and we become the means of sharing God's love to one another and to the world. In other words, we do not make, maintain, or save the church by our giving. Instead, we receive the church as God's gift and we participate in sharing that gift.

In response to this grace, the church is called to participate in God's generosity to the world. The mission of the church is our partnership in God's offering of Christ to all people. In so doing, the church provides opportunities for individual members to contribute to God's mission.

We give *to* and *through* the church as a spiritual practice. We give *to* the church as an expression of our spiritual fellowship. We give *through* the church to advance God's generosity to the world.

The generous church is a fellowship of believers who share one another's burdens and a partnership of disciples who work together for God's mission to the world.

How has the church helped you be a generous person?

When have you received the generosity (emotional, timely, or financial) of the church?

If the church is created, sustained, and renewed by God's grace, how should this shape the way we talk about the church's finances?

READINGS

Acts 4: 32-5:11

How was the church a "counter-cultural" community through its generosity?

What was the relationship between their generosity with one another and the apostles' message about the resurrection?

Why did Ananias and Sapphira die? What might this tell us about our spiritual relationship with our possessions?

2 Corinthians 8:1-15

What was the example of the church in Macedonia?

How was giving an expression of their spiritual connections?

According to Paul, why give?

Psalm 46

God promises protection and prosperity to Jerusalem. In similar ways, how has God provided for the church?

The psalm describes the city as a joyful refuge from a chaotic world. What kinds of economic "chaos" are people facing today?

How can the church be a joyful refuge for them?

CHURCH GENEROSITY AUDIT

Review your home church's relationships with other organizations and ministries, both with its official programs and informal relationships.

Rate each form of generosity on a scale from one to five (one = the church does very little; five = the church excels).

How many opportunities are there to engage in each:

Rating: *Opportunities:*

___ Emotional generosity _____

___ Timely generosity _____

___ Financial generosity _____

In what ways are you generous to and through the church?

For you, which type of generosity do you practice the most/least in the church?

GENEROSITY EXPERIMENT FOUR

If you are a part of a small group, Sunday school class or other group, plan one activity of generosity for your group to engage in during the next 60 days.

If you are not in a group, ask two other members to join you in planning and doing an act of generosity.

5. The Generous God

INTRODUCTION

The most illuminating part of Smith and Davidson's research is the worldview of ungenerous Americans (chapter 4).

Comparing interviews with ungenerous and generous persons, they saw stark differences in the outlooks of each group. Even though two people may have similar financial and personal circumstances, the ungenerous person will see "a world of scarcity, deficiency, vulnerability, and insecurity."

In turn, "personal autonomy, self-preservation, and rugged individualism are key and sacred concepts in the vocabulary of the ungenerous people" they interviewed[6].

In contrast, the persons they interviewed who practiced a generous lifestyle saw reality as infused with meaning and purpose, and saw possibilities and an abundance of blessings through their relationships.

The spiritual practice of generosity forces us to confront whether we see the world as one of scarcity or abundance. As long as one focuses on scarcity it will be difficult to practice generosity and to receive the benefits of a generous lifestyle.

Smith and Davidson counsel: "Practicing generosity often entails at some point an existential confrontation that is involved in the personal paradigm shift away from living in a world of scarcity and instead into living in a world of abundance, blessing, gratitude, enjoyment, security, and sharing. Therefore, practicing generosity in this way tends to promote happiness, health, and purposeful living."[7]

This paradigm shift is possible because of who God is. God is a generous God, and when you learn to see the world from the perspective of divine generosity you will be able to discover the fulfillment of generous living.

In religious terms, Smith and Davidson are talking about "repentance." Repentance is a mental, emotional and behavioral shift from one worldview to another. What makes this repentance possible is that God's generous love in Jesus Christ saturates our lives and the world.

This week we will examine the Christian story from the perspective of divine generosity. God created the world as a pure act of love, and God redeems the world as a free gift. As we prepare to go through Holy Week we will see how Jesus' final days, his death, and his resurrection are expressions of generosity that reshape the world.

READINGS

John 3:16-17 and Deuteronomy 8:11-18

What does the Exodus story tell us about the generosity of God?

Examine each stage of Jesus' life: birth, ministry, death, resurrection. How is each stage an expression of the generosity of God?

How is divine generosity the common thread that links John 3 and Deuteronomy 8?

How did people respond to God's generosity in Exodus and in the Gospels?

What are the Israelites commanded to remember when they become prosperous?

How does this memory shape our perspective and practice of generosity?

What do your practices of generosity imply about your view of God and reality?

GENEROSITY EXPERIMENT FIVE:
DEDICATION TO GENEROSITY

In this final exercise you will put together your personal vision of generosity and list specific practices that you will commit to do as part of your generous lifestyle.

My favorite scripture verse about generosity is:

In one sentence: "I am generous because…

By God's grace, I will....

Emotional generosity practice:

Timely generosity practice:

Financial generosity practice:

---

[1] p. 4.

[2] p. 11.

[3] p. 96.

[4] For the complete survey, see p. 18 of "The Paradox of Generosity."

[5] Timely generosity combines what Smith and Davidson categorize as "Neighborly Generosity" and "Volunteering."

[6] p. 74, 119.

[7] p. 77-78.

About the Author

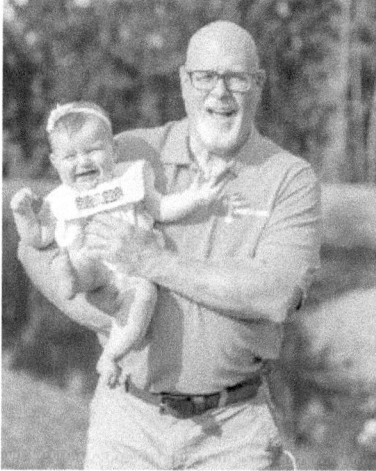

Darren Cushman Wood is the senior pastor of North United Methodist Church in Indianapolis, Indiana. He has served small and large, rural and urban United Methodist churches for over 30 years. He is a graduate of the University of Evansville and Union Theological Seminary.

He is the author of two books, hymns, and numerous articles. He is an adjunct professor of labor studies at Indiana University. He is married to Ginny and as of this writing they have three adult children and one grandchild.

The North Study Series

www.ingramcontent.com/pod-product-compliance
Lightning Source LLC
LaVergne TN
LVHW051207080426
835508LV00021B/2852